100 Things to do on a Car Journey

Sam Smith

Illustrated by Non Figg
and Molly Sage

Designed by Michael Hill
and Sharon Cooper

Edited by Sam Taplin

1

Store memories

Study the six stores on this street for 30 seconds, then cover them up and write the correct name of the store where you could buy the items below.

Through the campsite

Find the right trail to guide the yellow car to the yellow tent.

Supply trucks

Draw designs and pictures on the sides of these trucks to show what each one is transporting.

Games on the go

1. Use the letters in a vehicle plate to make up the silliest phrase you can think of. For example, you could say SDP is short for 'snails dance philosophically.'

2. Make up stories from a plate's letters. The first letter starts the name of your main character. The second is for what that character is doing. The third is for where they're doing it. So, **PFM** could start a story where Peter Pan **f**lies to the **M**oon.

3. Make up rhymes using the names on road signs you see. For example, 'On Station Road, I saw a toad!'

In the scrapyard

Help the man in the white T-shirt find his way
back to his friends who are fixing their car.

Picture code

Each picture below stands for a different number from 1 to 4. The numbers at the edges of the grid are the sum of the numbers in each row or column. Can you find out which picture represents which number?

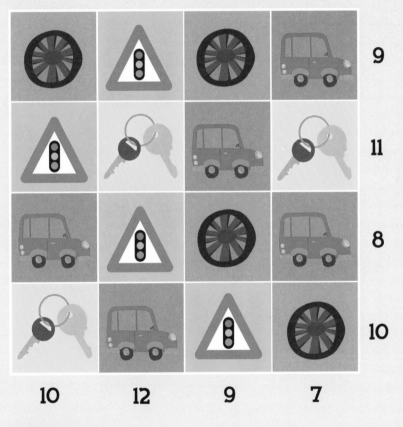

9

11

8

10

10   12   9   7

Answers:

 = ...   = ... 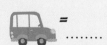 = ...   = ...

Desert rally

Which way must the jeep go to finish this desert rally?
It must stick to the trails made by the lighter sand.

· FINISH ·

Fill the field

Draw some more sheep grazing in this roadside field.

Driving quiz

1) Which city has over 10,000 yellow taxis?

a) London   b) New York   c) Paris

2) A dashboard was originally a board that protected people from the mud thrown up by their horses' hooves at high speed.

True or false?

3) Which country has the most road vehicles in the world?

a) China   b) Germany   c) USA

4) Which of these cities doesn't allow any cars on its streets?

a) Frankfurt   b) Venice   c) Marseilles

5) There are more cars than people in Los Angeles.

True or false?

6) Until 1896 in Britain, anyone who went for a drive had to have a man walk in front of their vehicle waving a red flag. Was he a...

a) policeman?   b) soldier?   c) judge?

Cops and robbers

Which is the getaway car? Help the police car find it by taking the road with the question that gives the lowest answer at each turn. Underline the correct car.

63-48=?

28÷2=?

4x4=?

13x4=?

60÷5=?

6x8=?

54-36=?

23+28=?

7x7=?

26+38=?

7x9=?

15x6=?

87-78=?

14x3=?

99-34=?

49+47=?

44÷4=?

12+27=?

Crossword 1

Use the clues below to put the correct words into the grid.

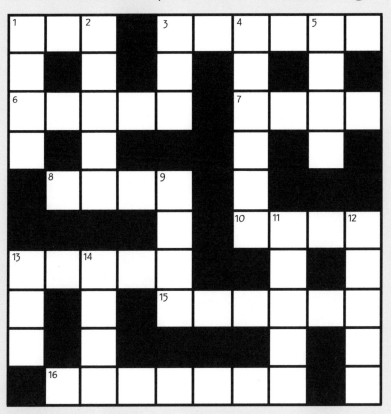

Across

1. Circuit of a track (3)
3. Speed competitors (6)
6. Helped (5)
7. Close, not far (4)
8. It stops water draining away (4)
10. 365 days (4)
13. A smell (5)
15. Keeper of a park; wanderer (6)
16. Go backwards in a car (7)

Down

1. To put things in or on a vehicle (4)
2. What a driver presses with their foot (5)
3. You have to stop at this light (3)
4. A group of vehicles in a line (6)
5. What a car travels on (4)
9. Toothed wheel in an engine (4)
11. Bird of prey (5)
12. In the countryside (5)
13. What you breathe (3)
14. A fairytale monster (4)

20 questions

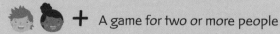 **+** A game for two or more people

1. One person thinks of something for everyone else to try to identify.

2. The other players take turns to ask a question about it – but no more than 20 questions can be asked in total. The questions can only be answered with 'Yes' or 'No' so they need to be things like 'Is it fluffy?' or 'Would you find it on a farm?'

3. If someone thinks they know what the thing is, they can guess at any time, but the guess counts as one of the 20 questions. If they are right, they have won, but if not, they are out of the game.

4. If no one guesses what it is by the time 20 questions have been asked, the person who thought of it has won.

Grid look

In the picture below, draw around the two groups of six cars that match the groups shown on the right.

Car words

Can you find these car words hidden in the sentences below? The first one has been done for you.

CARS

~~brake~~	wheel	gear	roof
pedal	window	seat	driver

1. The curious zebra kept following our car.

2. The sports car sped along the road.

3. I dipped my feet in the cold river water.

4. The hero often rides off into the sunset.

5. The police don't know how he eluded them.

6. We watched the sun rise at the cape.

7. The voyage around the island took all morning.

8. If we win, do we get a prize?

Road signs

Create your own symbols on these blank road signs,
or draw the ones you see on your journey.

Lap times

The board below shows the lap times of these cars during a four-lap race. Car D won the race by five seconds, but was two seconds behind the car that was leading at the end of lap two. Fill in the missing lap times below.

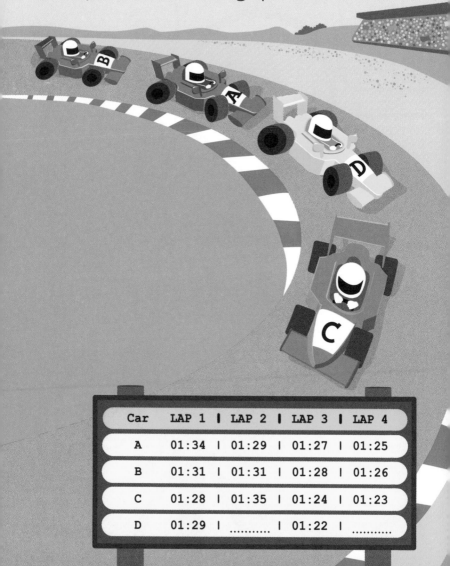

Car	LAP 1	LAP 2	LAP 3	LAP 4
A	01:34	01:29	01:27	01:25
B	01:31	01:31	01:28	01:26
C	01:28	01:35	01:24	01:23
D	01:29	....	01:22	....

Draw motorcars

Follow the steps below to draw some cars.

1. Draw a rectangle
and a roof.

2. Give the car
some windows.

3. Add wheels
and hubcaps.

4. Draw wheel
arches and lights.

Too many tools

Doug has used every tool in his box to fix his car this morning, and now he's feeling hungry. Guide him across his cluttered workshop to his lunch box for a well-earned lunch.

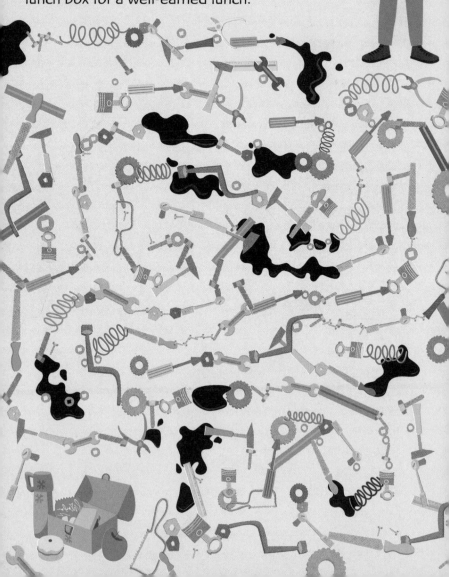

Highway hunt

Find all the different words for roads at the bottom in the grid. They may be written in any direction.

```
E R A F H G U O R O H T
T A E L U A L L O Y S E
R N V T U A R V M A N O
A D I D R I D R O A D L
L N R L I A V N L R A O
R T D A O T C T O L K H
E T H O V O E K D H R I
V Y E U N E V A A T E G
O L N A R U L L L G M H
Y U D T F R N U O L K W
L O S E T I T C O V E A
F B L I A R T S L B R Y
```

Avenue   Boulevard   Highway   Track

Alley   Street   Road   Thoroughfare

Drive   Lane   Trail   Flyover

Night drive

Draw some more outlines of buildings to finish
the view of this city's silhouetted skyline.

I spy

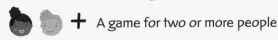 A game for two or more people

1. Look for something that everyone can see, but don't tell them what it is. (Try to pick something that you'll all be able to see for the next five minutes.)

2. Then say, 'I spy with my little eye, something beginning with...' followed by the first letter of what you've chosen.

3. Everyone else takes turns to guess things they can see that start with that letter. Whoever guesses what it is thinks of the next one.

Another idea: Instead of giving the first letter as a clue, you could say something like, 'I spy with my little eye, something... green.' Or 'I spy with my little eye, something... smelly.'

Symbol sudoku

This grid is made up of six blocks, each made up of six squares. Fill in the blank squares so that every row, column and block contains all six of the symbols shown below.

Back and forth

1. Circle the car two in front of the car behind the car in front of the car two behind the blue car.

2. Circle the car behind the car in front of the car in front of the car two behind the car in front of the red car.

3. Circle the car that's behind the car two behind the car in front of the car in front of the purple car.

Traffic doodle

Turn all the shapes below into lots of vehicles on the road.

Signpost scramble

Can you unscramble the letters on each of the signs
below to find the names of ten places in this town?

1. SUEMUM

2. APORE USHEO

3. TONSIAT

4. ILBARRY

5. GNOPPISH LALM

6. MUSIDAT

7. LOOP

8. KREMAT

9. KPRA

10. LARGELY

Country park

Guide the red car along a clear route down these country roads to the parking area.

WELCOME

Famous drivers

Find the famous Formula One drivers at the bottom hidden in the grid. Their names may be written in any direction.

```
N E S F A D U A L S O M
T G R M A N S E L L G P
E Y T T E Q N P M A T O
Q N S N A I S E N U A P
O N O L I R A C S A E I
I O R T A F A L I L T Q
G F P N L D L F L N O U
N A G Q I I N S Q I P E
A R C N H L M E S G R T
F P I L T O N A O O N O
A D R E R I M C H C M D
M E O S N O L A D A R I
```

Lauda   Moss

Fangio   Hamilton

Senna   Mansell   Hill

Prost   Alonso   Piquet   Ascari

Parallel roads

Draw an X on the road that runs parallel to the road that the truck is on.

Snapshot spot

Can you spot seven differences between these two rally-car photos?

Who lives there?

 ✛ A game for two or more people

One person looks around for an unusual or interesting looking house. When they see one, they ask 'Who lives there?' Everyone takes turns describing who the owners might be.

Age?

Pets?

Dark secret?

Big family?

Haunted?

Job?

Trailers and roof racks

Give each of these cars a roof rack on top or a trailer to tow.

Crossword 2

Use the clues below to put the correct words into the grid.

Across

1. Pointed at a target (5)
4. Huge; giant (4)
6. Playing ____; greetings ____ (5)
7. Wet weather (4)
8. It opens a lock (3)
10. What you do in a 2 down (4)
11. Throttle; gag (5)
12. Danger (4)
13. Set fire to (4)
16. Neat, orderly (4)
18. Places to buy in a market (6)

Down

1. Go faster and faster (10)
2. What drivers use to see behind (7)
3. Twilight (4)
4. Really; to a great extent (4)
5. Slid sideways on slippery ground (7)
9. Pipe at the back of a car; tire out (7)
14. Zero, none (3)
15. Large road vehicle with many seats (3)
17. Perform an action (2)

Travel sudoku

The grid below is made up of six blocks, each made up of six squares. Fill in the blank squares so that every row, column and block contains all six letters of the word TRAVEL.

L			T	A	
T			E	L	
	V	R			L
	L	T			E

Workshop wheels

This car is in the workshop to be fitted with four new wheels.
Can you find a set of four identical ones in the pile below?

Road timeline

Label these road inventions with numbers 1 to 6 to put them in historical order, using 1 for the earliest.

Horse-drawn bus

Cat's eye reflector

Road bridge

Roman milestone

Traffic lights

Road glow strips

Quick draw

Draw a line as fast as you can from the broken-down car to the end of its smoke plume, without touching the sides.

Chauffeur

Draw a face on your chauffeur and give him a name.

Supermarket dash

Find a clear route through the town to buy some groceries
before the supermarket shuts.

Trip to the zoo

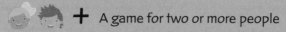 ✛ A game for two or more people

1. One player begins by saying, 'On our trip to the zoo, I saw...' followed by the name of an animal. For example, 'On our trip to the zoo, I saw a gorilla.'

2. The next player must repeat what the first player said, then add another animal, so they might say, 'On our trip to the zoo, I saw a gorilla and a giraffe.'

3. Each turn, that player must list all of the animals that have already been said, and in the correct order, before saying another, different animal that they saw.

4. The game ends when someone forgets an animal, or says them in the wrong order.

Another idea: You could also say how many of each animal you saw to make the game harder. For example, 'On our trip to the zoo, I saw eight gorillas, six giraffes and two tigers.'

In the garage

Three cars are parked in these garages. Following the clues below, can you find out the owner of each car, its age, and whether it's painted red, green or blue? Fill in your answers on the chart.

Last driven	Owner	R/G/B	Age
Wednesday			
Thursday			
Friday			

1. The green car is 5 years older than the blue car, and isn't owned by Andrew.

2. The car that was last driven on Thursday is 10 years younger than the red car, which is owned by Paul.

3. The owner of the car that's 5 years old isn't Clive, who last drove his car on Wednesday.

4. The blue car is 5 years old.

Rainbow race

Five cars were in a race. *Yellow* finished before *Red* but after *Orange*. *Green* wasn't first, but finished two places in front of *Blue*. The car that finished last had no stripes. Write the correct finishing position on each of the cars.

Draw a truck

Follow the steps below to draw a truck, then fill the page with more of them.

1. Draw these shapes.

2. Add three wheels.

3. Add cables and a driver's window.

Cityscape

Finish this scene by adding details to the cars and buildings.

One beat only

 + A game for two or more people

Some words have just one 'beat' in them. For example, all of the words in the previous sentence just have one 'beat' – a beat in a word is known as a syllable.

Now, look for something out of the window and try to describe it to the other players, using words with just one syllable and without saying the thing itself, so they can guess what it is.

For example, if you saw a frog in a pond, you could say:

'It lives in a pond. It hops and it likes to eat flies.'

Another idea: You could try having a whole conversation with someone about anything you like, using words of just one syllable. See how long you can keep it up.

Muddy recovery

Starting at the bottom, follow the chains to see which car the tow truck is pulling out of the deep mud first.

Stunt search

Find the names of the driving moves and stunts at the bottom hidden in the grid, written in any direction.

```
E S U R W H E E L I E N S
T D C E H R E U T J H R S
L F S O R E V N R O K U A
O L I Z R E I D H T C T P
N R O H L K O B A F A E T
I R B R S R S R S I B K O
B Z U P T E O C L R N A H
S U I T H S O F R D C R S
L N R D J R Z T B E T B G
H P O N W H E E L O W D N
A J T U O T O O B E H N I
E B E S P U J Y Z E E A L
R E G G E L T O O B H H S
```

SKI

DRIFT

BURNOUT

HANDBRAKE TURN

J-TURN

HEEL-TOE SHIFT

SLINGSHOT PASS

SPIN

WHEELIE

CORKSCREW

BOOTLEGGER

Signpost squares

Write all the numbers 1 to 9 in the grid, so the four squares around each circle add up to the circle's total, and the red, green and blue squares add up to the totals shown at the bottom. One number has been filled in for you.

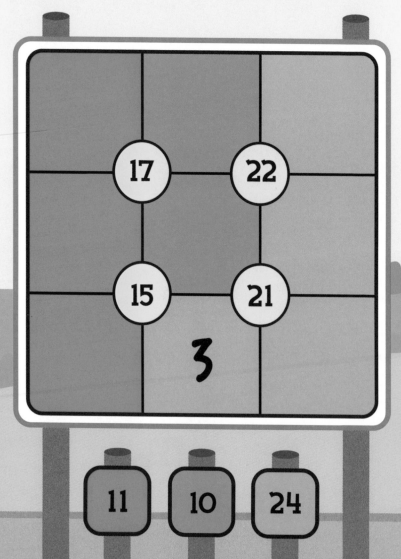

Road trip

Add some designs to these camping vehicles.

Traffic jam

Study these vehicles, then try to match each one to a silhouette on the opposite page.

1

2

3

4

5

6

7

8

9

10

11

12

13

14

15

Write the correct number next to each letter.

A ....

B...........

C...........

D ....

E...........

F ....

G...........

H...........

I...........

J...........

K...........

L ....

M...........

N...........

O...........

Track words

Find a word that can *go* after the word on the left and in front of the word on the right to make two new words.

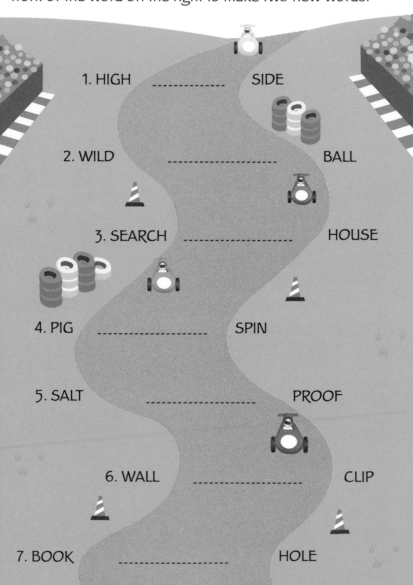

1. HIGH .... SIDE

2. WILD .... BALL

3. SEARCH .... HOUSE

4. PIG .... SPIN

5. SALT .... PROOF

6. WALL .... CLIP

7. BOOK .... HOLE

Half car

Draw the *other half* of this car, then add a driver and a passenger, a registration number, and other final details.

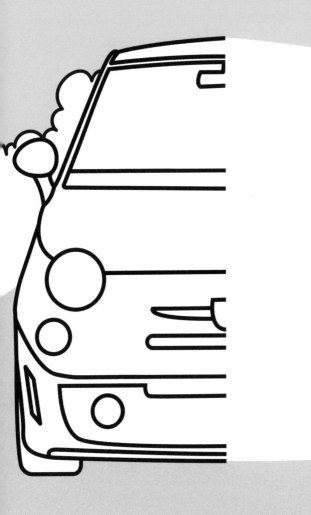

True or false?

For each of the statements below, circle 'T' if you think
it's true, or 'F' if you think it's false.

1. Ferruccio Lamborghini was a successful manufacturer
of tractors before he switched to sports cars.   **T / F**

2. Formula One drivers lose weight each time they race.
T / F

3. More Model-T Fords were sold than any other car
in history.   **T / F**

4. There is a limousine that has a swimming pool and a
helicopter landing pad.   **T / F**

5. In Australia, motorists drive on the right-hand side
of the road.   **T / F**

6. The German inventor Rudolf Diesel designed and
built the first internal combustion engine.   **T / F**

7. Scientists have built a mind-controlled car.   **T / F**

8. In Russia, it is against the law to drive a dirty car.
T / F

Woodland words

Steer the car through the forest. You must always choose the clearing whose word is next in alphabetical order.

BYE

scooter

tricycle

motorcycle

rickshaw

tractor

taxi

moped

limousine

car

go-kart

jeep

bus

bicycle

minibus

WELCOME

coach

automobile

Through the gears

Add arrows to show which way gears B and C are turning.

54

A

B

C

Tongue twisters

Try to say each of these tongue twisters as fast as you can, or challenge some of your fellow passengers.

1. A proper cup of coffee from a proper copper coffee pot.

2. Wun-wun was a racehorse, Tutu was one too,
   Wun-wun won one race, Tutu won one too.

3. Black background, brown background...

4. A tutor who tooted the flute,
   Tried to tutor two tooters to toot.
   Said the two to the tutor:
   'Is it harder to toot, or
   To tutor two tooters to toot?'

5. Five frantic frogs fled from fifty fiercely flailing fishes.

6. A loyal warrior will rarely worry why we rule.

7. Betty bought a bit of butter, but the bit of butter Betty bought was bitter, so Betty bought a bit of better butter to make the bitter bit of butter better.

Hidden picture

Fill in all the shapes that have red dots. What can you see?

Traffic trouble

Can you find a way through the traffic to cross this very busy road? (Luckily, all the vehicles have stopped.)

Start
here

Vehicle find-it

Find all of the vehicles below hidden in the grid.
Their names may be written in any direction.

AMBULANCE   LIMO   JEEP   BUS

MOTORCYCLE   TAXI   TRUCK   CARAVAN

CONVERTIBLE   TRACTOR   CAR   BICYCLE

```
E E L B I T R E V N O C
C A R C H T P N P E E J
N E B R E C A N O E H S
A N L S D N S L O L C U
L R C C D A A T Y C A B
U O T A Y E A L M Y R T
B T A A H C P A P C A N
M C P B X O I O A R V E
A A A Y Y I M B C O A V
Y R N A C I C L N T N N
N T E A L O D N O O S O
A T K C U R T Y A M A C
```

Twin tractors

Circle the two tractor-and-trailers below that are identical.

Sudoku

The grid below is made up of nine blocks, each containing nine squares. Fill in the blank squares so that every block, row and column contains all the digits 1 to 9.

	1		5				2	9
9			1			3		
2	5		9		8			
	3			1		4	7	
7			4	8	6			3
	9	1		5			8	
			6		1		3	2
		2			7			4
6	4				5		9	

Designer vehicles

Add designs to all of the
vehicles below.

Squiggle shapes

Turn these squiggles into things you might see on a journey.

Car-part scramble

Can you unscramble these letters to find the names of five different parts of a car?

1. presilo = ...

2. suxheat = ...

3. badhoards = ...

4. ragabis = ...

5. ghilst = ...

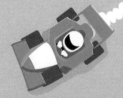

Car snap

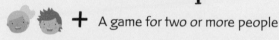 A game for two or more people

The aim of this game is to spot pairs of cars or other vehicles, such as trucks and motorcycles, that are both seen at the same time, or within a short time limit.

• For an easy game, look for, say, two blue cars, or two silver cars, that are both in view at the same time.

• For a harder game, try to spot two vehicles that are also the same type, such as two red sports cars, two green trucks and so on, within five minutes of each other.

• For an even harder game, try to spot two vehicles that are exactly the same model, too, in a five-minute window.

Whoever manages to spot the most pairs is the winner.

Draw a monster truck

Follow the steps below to draw a monster truck, then fill the page below with as many as you can fit in.

 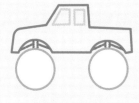 

1. Draw the truck's body and two large wheels.

2. Add windows and suspension.

3. Add designs and wheel grip.

Broken down

Which oil leak will lead Dave the mechanic to the broken-down car so he can fix it?

Winning total

Find each car's total to see how quickly they will get around the track. The one with the lowest total will finish first. Circle the winner.

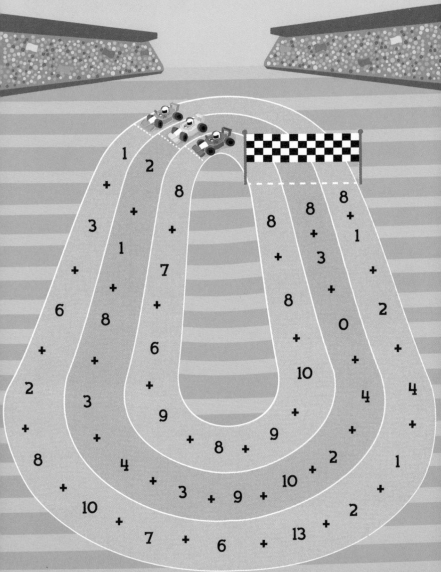

1 + 3 + 6 + 2 + 8 + 10 + 7

2 + 1 + 8 + 3 + 4 + 3 + 6

8 + 7 + 6 + 9 + 8 + 9 + 9

8 + 8 + 3 + 8 + 10 + 2 + 10 + 13

8 + 1 + 2 + 4 + 1 + 2

Car parts

Circle the group of parts that
can be put together to make
up the car shown on the right.

A

B

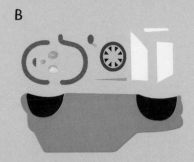

C

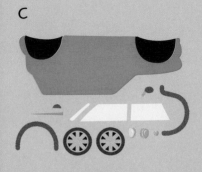

D

E

F

Car conundrums

1. A man who'd just been released from jail was pushing his car when he stopped in front of a hotel, and declared himself bankrupt. What was he doing?

Answer: ....

2. A taxi driver didn't like people talking to him when he was working. When his latest passenger started chatting to him, he didn't respond, and when she tapped him on the shoulder he shouted, "Sorry, I can't hear a thing!" However, when she arrived home, she knew he'd lied. Can you explain how?

Answer: ....

3. Can you work out the number of the space that the car below is parked in?

Answer: ....

Crossword 3

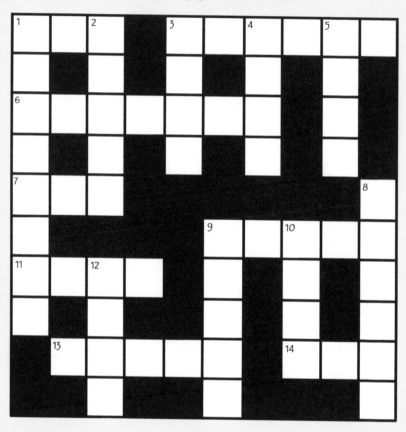

Across

1. Slippery liquid (3)
3. Black road surface (6)
6. These make vehicles go (7)
7. Disapproving noise (3)
9. Opposite of higher (5)
11. Hit with your foot (4)
13. What you use to stop (5)
14. Oxygen, for example (3)

Down

1. Go past another vehicle (8)
2. It illuminates (5)
3. A container for liquid (4)
4. Hurry (4)
5. What a wheel turns on (4)
8. Drive smoothly; boat journey (6)
9. Little roads; sections of a road (5)
10. Side of a vehicle; part of a plane (4)
12. Automobiles (4)

Busy campsite

The red car has just arrived at this campsite. Fill it with more tents, then draw designs on the canvases and add guy ropes and tent pegs.

Fizzbuzz

 + A game for two or more people

1. Everyone takes turns to say numbers, counting up to 100. So, the first player starts by saying 'one' the next player says 'two' and so on.

2. When it's a player's turn to say a number that can be divided by **three**, they must say **'fizz'** instead of that number.

3. If a player would say a number that can be divided by **five**, they must say **'buzz'** instead of that number.

4. When a number can be divided by both **three and five**, the player whose turn it is must say **'fizzbuzz'**.

5. If a player makes a mistake, they drop out of the game. The last person left counting is the winner. If there's more than one player left when you reach 100, it's a draw.

Tower trace

Draw along the outline of the Eiffel Tower, starting at the blue arrow, and without taking your pencil off the page.

Plate mix-up

Can you unscramble the car-related words on these plates?

1. MORRRIS

2. EDEPS

3. KERABS

4. EENING

5. RHNO

Racing quiz

1) Who is the only driver to have won seven Formula One world championships?

a) Ayrton Senna   b) Lewis Hamilton   c) Michael Schumacher

2) Which race is sometimes known as 'The Greatest Spectacle in Racing': the Monaco Grand Prix **or** the Indianapolis 500?

3) How long does the sports car endurance race held every year at Le Mans, France last?

a) 6 hours   b) 12 hours   c) 24 hours

4) What was the name of the vehicle that Donald Campbell drove to break the land speed record in 1964:
Bluebird **or** *Green Monster*?

5) Which flag is used to stop a motor race before the end?

a) yellow flag   b) red flag   c) blue flag

6) Which of these races does NOT involve cars?

a) Tour de France   b) Dakar Rally   c) Gumball 3000

Quick draw

Draw a line as fast as you can from the car to the service station, without leaving the road.

Custom keyring

Decorate these keyrings, then draw some more.

Cross sum

Fill in the blank squares with numbers from 1 to 9. The numbers in each row or column should add up to the total shown on the arrows. (The direction of the arrows shows you whether to add across or down the grid.) You can only use a number once in an answer. For example, you can make 4 with 3 and 1, but not with 2 and 2.

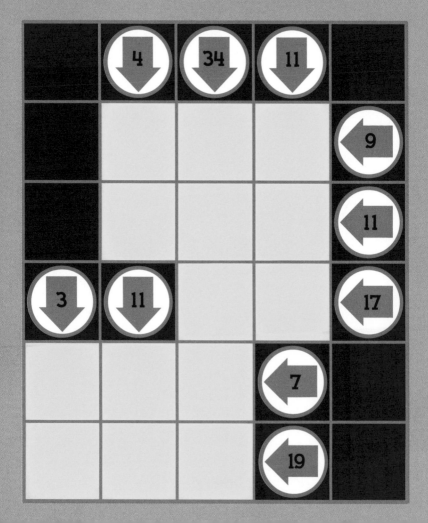

Kart race

Guide the kart along a
clear route to the finish
as fast as you can.

Start

Pit stop

Finish

Draw a bus

Follow the steps below to draw a bus, then fill the page with buses.

1. Draw this shape.

2. Add windows for passengers.

3. Draw wheels and a driver's window.

USBORNE PUBLISHING

Who am I?

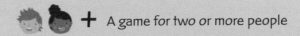 **+** A game for two or more people

1. One player thinks of a person that everyone will know, for example, Sleeping Beauty or Santa Claus.

I'm Santa Claus!

I have a white beard – who am I?

2. They then give the others a clue, like this:

'I'm in a fairy tale – who am I?'

Each person has one guess. If someone gets it right, it is their turn to think of a person for the others to guess. If no one guesses correctly, the first person gives another clue:

'I have royal parents – who am I?'

3. The game continues until someone guesses the mystery person, or until ten clues have been given. If no one gets it right, the first person tells everyone who it was, then thinks of someone else for them to guess.

Race eighteen

Label the blank racing cars with the remaining numbers from 2 to 10 so that each row, column and diagonal line of three adds up to 18. No number can be used twice.

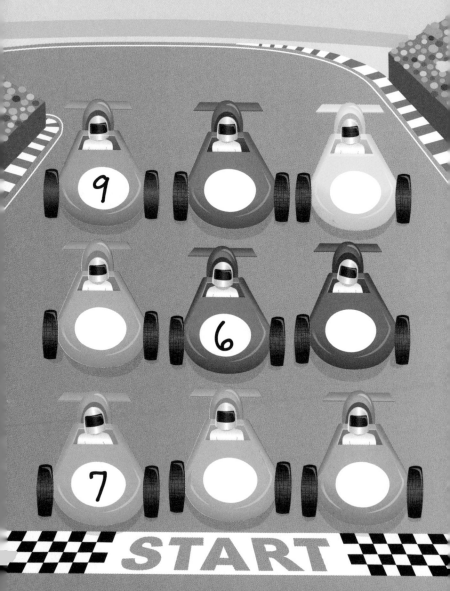

Motor maze

Steer the blue car between the hedgerows
to reach the house in the middle
of this maze.

Drive-in quiz

1) Which of these cars has NOT been one of 007's cars in a James Bond movie?
a) Jaguar
b) Aston Martin
c) Lotus

2) Which car famously featured as the getaway vehicle in the movie *The Italian Job*?
a) Fiat Topolino   b) Mini Cooper   c) Ford Fiesta

3) Who was a Wacky Racer, always dressed in bright pink?
a) Charlotte Chicane
b) Lucy Laptime
c) Penelope Pitstop

4) Who is the main character in the Disney movie *Cars*:
Greased Lightning **or** Lightning McQueen?

5) Which car transforms into a boat, and also has wings and propellers so it can fly?
a) Herbie
b) The Batmobile
c) Chitty Chitty Bang Bang

Grid upgrade

Draw another car on the grid, exactly the same shape but twice as big. The first part has been done for you.

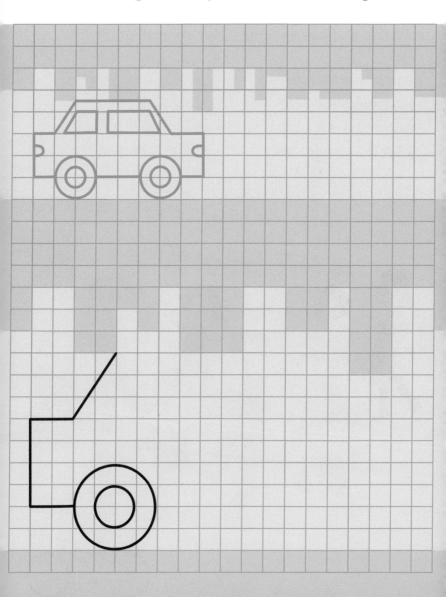

Scavenger hunt

Look out of the window. Can you spot people doing all of the things on the list below? Try to spot one of each thing before the end of your journey. Or you could play against someone and see who can spot them all first.

- carrying a newspaper
- walking a dog
- wearing a hat
- wearing sunglasses
- carrying shopping bags
- riding a bicycle
- walking with a baby
- eating or drinking

Tricky traffic

Find out what the cars on each road have in common, then choose the car that follows each pattern. Write their numbers in the empty circles.

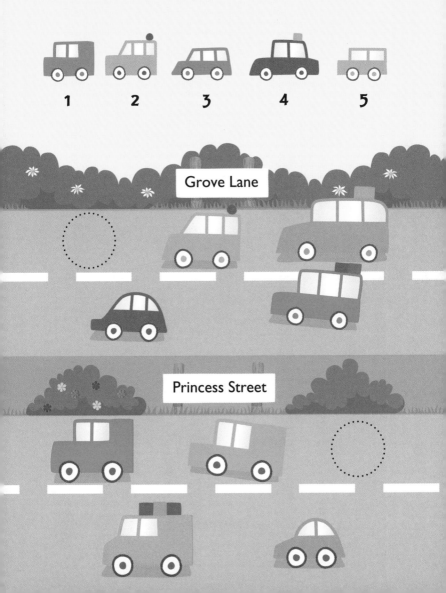

Rally route

Which route must the rally car follow through the forest to reach the finish?

Finish

Cloudy cars

Transform these cloud shapes into funny cars in the sky.

Car calculations

Draw spots on 20% of the cars below.

Then, draw squares on 25% of the cars left blank.

Next, draw stripes on one third of the blank cars.

Lastly, draw swirls on half of the cars still left blank.

How many blank cars are there now?

ANSWER . . . .

Manufacturers quiz

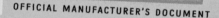

OFFICIAL MANUFACTURER'S DOCUMENT

1) Who is credited with successfully building the first car: Karl Benz **or** Gottlieb Daimler?

2) Which car manufacturer's symbol does NOT feature a prancing horse?
a) Ferrari   b) Porsche   c) Lamborghini

3) What was the world's first car built using a moving assembly line?
a) VW Beetle   b) Ford Model-T   c) Peugeot 201

4) Which city in America is known as the heart of the country's automotive industry?
a) Chicago   b) Detroit   c) Seattle

5) What was the name of the Rolls-Royce engine that powered the Supermarine Spitfire and some other British planes in the Second World War?
a) Dumbledore   b) Gandalf   c) Merlin

6) Which famous American outlaw wrote to Henry Ford to compliment him on his cars:
Clyde Barrow **or** John Dillinger?

Bus tour

The red bus is touring Santa Mona, driving past all the sights, before arriving at the hotel. The tour buses never retrace any of their route. Which way will the bus *go*?

Last answer

 A game for two people

1. One person asks a really easy question, such as 'Where can you find moondust?' The other person doesn't answer.

2. The first person then asks another easy question, such as 'Where does your grandma live?' The second person doesn't answer that question, but has to answer the first one – in this example: 'On the moon.'

3. The game continues with the first person asking questions and the other answering them, always one question behind.

4. The game ends when the second person answers the wrong question. Then it is that player's turn to ask the questions.

TIP: Try to ask questions so that the answer to the previous question sounds like a really silly answer to the one you've just asked.

Map maker

Make a map of your journey, drawing anything of interest you see along the way, starting at your house.

My house

One of these cars is on its way to the sea, one is going to the airport, and one is going to the city. Follow the compass directions below to find out where each car goes, and the route it takes to get there.

N = North   E = East   S = South   W = West

  E E E S S S W S S E E S S S E E S S E E S E E N

  E E S E E E N E E N E S S E E S S W S S E E S W W W S W N W N N

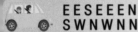 E E S W S E E E N E E N E S E E E E S S W W W S S W S S W W S W W N W N

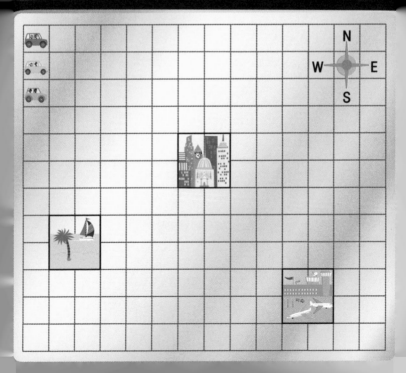

Eyes on the road

Draw what you can see from the front of your car.

Café visit

These friends have had lunch at the
Maze Café and now they need to get
back to their cars. Find out which way
they should go.

Vehicle shapes

Turn all of the shapes below into different things that go.

Jumbled junctions

The car that drives under the most bridges will reach the
rail bridge first. Which will it be?

Key match-up

Circle the two sets of keys that can be turned so that they match each other exactly.

Answers

2. Through the campsite:

5. In the scrapyard:

6. Picture code:

= 2   = 4

= 1   = 3

7. Desert rally:

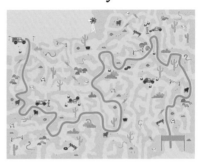

9. Driving quiz:

1. b 2. True 3. c 4. b (Venice's streets are very narrow as its canals are people's main means of transport.) 5. True 6. a

10. Cops and robbers:

11. Crossword 1:

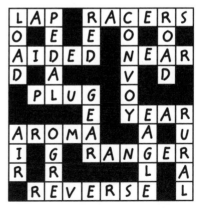

L	A	P		R	A	C	E	R	S
O		E		E		O		O	
A	I	D	E	D		N	E	A	R
D		A				V		D	
	P	L	U	G		O			
				E		Y	E	A	R
A	R	O	M	A			A		U
I		G		R	A	N	G	E	R
R		R				L			A
	R	E	V	E	R	S	E		L

Answers

13. Grid look:

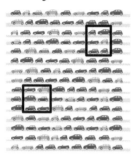

14. Car words:

1. The curious *zebra kept* following our car.

2. The sports car *sped along* the road.

3. I dipped my feet in the cold *river* water.

4. The *hero often* rides off into the sunset.

5. The police don't know *how he* eluded them.

6. We watched the sun *rise at* the cape.

7. The voyage *around* the island took all morning.

8. If we *win, do* we get a prize?

16. Lap times:

Lap 2: 01:35   Lap 4: 01:19

18. Too many tools:

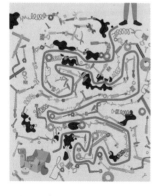

19. Highway hunt:

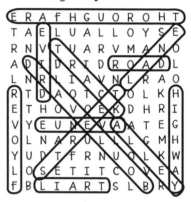

22. Symbol sudoku:

23. Back and forth:

1. blue 2. orange 3. pink

25. Signpost scramble:

1. museum 2. opera house
3. station 4. library 5. shopping
mall 6. stadium 7. pool
8. market 9. park 10. gallery

Answers

26. Country park:

27. Famous drivers:

28. Parallel roads: C

29. Snapshot spot:

32. Crossword 2:

33. Travel sudoku:

L	E	V	T	A	R
V	A	L	R	E	T
T	R	A	E	L	V
E	V	R	A	T	L
R	T	E	L	V	A
A	L	T	V	R	E

34. Workshop wheels:

Answers

35. Road timeline:

1. Road bridge
2. Roman milestone
3. Horse-drawn bus
4. Traffic lights
5. Cat's eye reflector
6. Road glow strips

38. Supermarket dash:

40. In the garage:

Last driven	Owner	R/G/B	Age
Wednesday	Clive	Green	10
Thursday	Andrew	Blue	5
Friday	Paul	Red	15

41. Rainbow race:

1. Orange 2. Yellow 3. Green
4. Red 5. Blue

45. Muddy recovery: C

46. Stunt search:

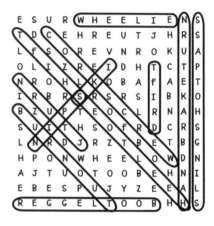

47. Signpost squares:

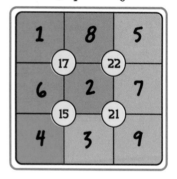

49. Traffic jam:

A9, B8, C6, D11, E12, F14, G10,
H2, I1, J15, K4, L5, M3, N7, O13

50. Track words:

1. way 2. fire 3. light 4. tail
5. water 6. paper 7. worm

Answers

52. True or false?:
1. T 2. T (due to high G-forces and temperatures) 3. F (the VW Beetle has sold more)
4. T 5. F 6. F 7. T 8. T

53. Woodland words:

54. Through the gears:

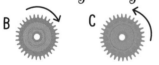

B   C

56. Hidden picture:

57. Traffic trouble:

58. Vehicle find-it:

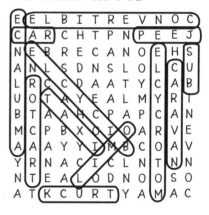

59. Twin tractors:

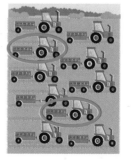

Answers

60. Sudoku:

3	1	8	5	6	4	7	2	9
9	6	4	1	7	2	3	5	8
2	5	7	9	3	8	6	4	1
8	3	6	2	1	9	4	7	5
7	2	5	4	8	6	9	1	3
4	9	1	7	5	3	2	8	6
5	7	9	6	4	1	8	3	2
1	8	2	3	9	7	5	6	4
6	4	3	8	2	5	1	9	7

70. Crossword 3:

O	I	L		T	A	R	M	A	C
V		I	A		U			X	
E	N	G	I	N	E	S		L	
R		H		K		H		E	
T	U	T							C
A				L	O	W	E	R	
K	I	C	K		A		I		U
E		A			N		N		I
	B	R	A	K	E		G	A	S
		S			S				E

63. Car-part scramble:

1. spoiler 2. exhaust 3. dashboard
4. airbags 5. lights

66. Broken down: B

67. Winning total:

68. Car parts: C

69. Car conundrums:

1. He was playing Monopoly.
2. Because she'd arrived at her destination, so he must have heard her when she said where she wanted to go.
3. 87 - the numbers are upside down as you look at them.

74. Plate mix-up:

1. mirrors 2. speed 3. brakes
4. engine 5. horn

75. Racing quiz:

1. c 2. the Indianapolis 500
3. c 4. *Bluebird* 5. b 6. a

78. Cross sum:

Answers

79. Kart race:

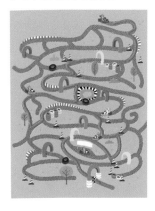

82. Race eighteen:

83. Motor maze:

84. Drive-in quiz:
1. a (None that has appeared in the movies has been Bond's car.)
2. b 3. c 4. Lightning McQueen
5. c

85. Grid upgrade:

87. Tricky traffic:
Grove Lane: 3
Princess Street: 4

88. Rally route:

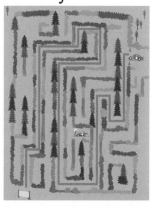

Answers

90. Car calculations:
Two blank cars

91. Manufacturers quiz:
1. Karl Benz 2. c 3. b 4. b
5. c 6. Clyde Barrow

92. Bus tour:

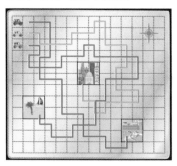

95. On the road:

97. Café visit:

99. Jumbled junctions:
The blue car

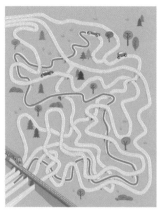

100. Key match-up: B and F

With thanks to Candice Whatmore and Lizzie Barber